PRESENTED TO

PRESENTED BY

DATE

PROVERBS
FOR LIFE™

for

Moms

Ψ

inspirio™

Proverbs for Life™ for Moms
ISBN 0-310-80189-3

Copyright © 2004 by GRQ Ink, Inc.
Franklin, Tennessee 37067
"Proverbs for Life" is a trademark owned by GRQ, Inc.

Published by Inspirio™, The gift group of Zondervan
5300 Patterson Avenue, SE
Grand Rapids, Michigan 49530

Requests for information should be addressed to:
Inspirio™, The gift group of Zondervan
Grand Rapids, Michigan 49530
http://www.inspiriogifts.com

Compiler: Lila Empson
Associate Editor: Janice Jacobson
Project Manager: Tom Dean
Manuscript written by Vicki Kuyper, Betsy Williams, Therese Stenzel, and Rebecca Currington in conjunction with Snapdragon Editorial Group, Inc.
Design: Whisner Design Group

03 04 05/HK/ 4 3 2 1

I

If you call out for insight

and cry aloud for understanding . . .

wisdom will enter your heart,

and knowledge will be

pleasant to your soul.

PROVERBS 2:3,10 NIV

Contents

Introduction

The book of Proverbs contains the timeless wisdom each person needs to live a happy, healthy, well balanced life—each entry teaching a practical principle designed to encourage good choices and positive problem solving.

Proverbs for Life™ for Moms takes those valuable principles and applies them to the issues you care about most—such as family, health, peace, and commitment. As you read through these pages, may you find the practical answers—God's answers—to the questions you are asking.

When good people pray, the LORD listens.

— *Proverbs 15:29* GNT

A Mother's Prayer

The only crown I ask,

dear Lord, to wear

Is this—that I may teach a little child.

I do not ask that I should ever stand

Among the wise, the worthy, or the great;

I only ask that softly, hand in hand,

A child and I may enter at your gate.

Author Unknown

WE'LL TALK LATER

Whoever is slow to anger has great understanding.

~ *Proverbs 14:29* NRSV

THE TWO BEST TIMES TO KEEP YOUR MOUTH SHUT ARE WHEN YOU'RE SWIMMING AND WHEN YOU'RE ANGRY.

AUTHOR UNKNOWN

Katie felt relief, thanksgiving, and exhaustion flow through her body as the headlights of her son Jeff's car flashed through the window. She noted the time—1:45 A.M. She had spent the past few hours pacing and praying, trying desperately to shake off her increasing anxiety. But now that she knew Jeff was safe, she could feel her angry rise. Almost two hours late—no call and most likely no excuse. *Why does he think he can do this every time his father is out of town?*

As her seventeen-year-old came through the door, Katie prayed for wisdom and calm.

"Hey Mom, sorry I'm late, I—"

"We'll talk in the morning," Katie responded. Previous confrontations had accomplished nothing. It was time to find a better way.

The next day, Katie and Jeff did have a talk. The intervening hours had given Jeff an opportunity to consider his actions and Katie a chance to choose her words wisely and come up with a well-considered consequence.

10

Being a mom is as difficult as it is wonderful. The feelings of concern, anxiety, and frustration generated by your children's behaviors can overwhelm you, leading to angry confrontations and words better left unsaid. But God has promised to show you how to respond in ways that will foster long-lasting results. First, though, you must wait for the calm that only His Spirit can bring.

TRY THIS: *The next time your child gives you reason to lose your temper or blow a fuse, impose a cooling-off period for yourself as well as for your child. Don't drop the issue, but use the time to pray that God will help you frame a wise and persuasive response.*

BE CAREFUL WHAT YOU SAY AND PROTECT YOUR LIFE. A CARELESS TALKER DESTROYS HIMSELF.

PROVERBS 13:3 GNT

HE THAT IS SLOW TO ANGER IS BETTER THAN THE MIGHTY; AND HE THAT RULETH HIS SPIRIT THAN HE THAT TAKETH A CITY.

PROVERBS 16:32 KJV

If you are patient in one moment of anger, you will avoid one hundred days of sorrow.

ANCIENT PROVERB

11

Out of the Driver's Seat

The human mind may devise many plans, but it is the purpose of the LORD that will be established.

— *Proverbs* 19:21 NRSV

Sandra had dreams for her children's lives, and she wanted Josh and Julie to be happy and successful. So when Josh decided to forego college and enlist in the Navy, she was concerned.

"Lord, I've always believed that you love my children even more than I do," she prayed. "Can this path really be right for Josh?"

As Sandra saw her son off, her eyes filled with tears but her heart filled with the peace only God can give a mother.

Soon after, Julie confided that she dreamed of becoming a missionary nurse and serving in the Congo. "Oh, but honey," Sandra replied, "I always thought you would want—"

"Mom, this is what God wants, too. I'm certain of that," Julie assured her.

In time, Sandra came to see that while her plans for Josh and Julie were born of love, they had little to do with God's will for their lives. Only he knew how to direct them onto the path to true success.

As a mother, you have dreams for your children. Relinquishing your dreams to God is the strongest test of faith you will ever face. But it is a test you must pass if your children are to become all they were meant to be, all God created them to be. By releasing your grip on their lives, you free them to accomplish God's perfect will.

Try this: *When you pray for your children, instead of reinforcing your own dreams and wishes, seek God's dreams and wishes for them. Try praying Scripture. Consider Jeremiah 29:11: "I alone know the plans I have for you, plans to bring you prosperity and not disaster, plans to bring about the future you hope for" (GNT).*

THERE IS NO WISDOM, NO INSIGHT, NO PLAN THAT CAN SUCCEED AGAINST THE LORD.

PROVERBS 21:30 NIV

"FOR MY THOUGHTS ARE NOT YOUR THOUGHTS, NEITHER ARE YOUR WAYS MY WAYS," DECLARES THE LORD. "AS THE HEAVENS ARE HIGHER THAN THE EARTH, SO ARE MY WAYS HIGHER THAN YOUR WAYS AND MY THOUGHTS THAN YOUR THOUGHTS."

ISAIAH 55:8-9 NIV

Inside the will of God there is no failure.
Outside the will of God there is no success.

BENARD EDINGER

A Mother's Faith

Faith is not in understanding;
Faith is yielding to God's will,
Resting on His Word of Promise
In assurance calm and still.

Faith is looking unto Jesus,
Trusting where it cannot see,
Faith is resting on His Promise.
Faith is glorious victory.

Avis B. Christiansen

One who trusts in the
LORD is secure.

— *Proverbs 29:25* NRSV

Faith is the substance
of things hoped for, the
evidence of things
not seen.

— *Hebrews 11:1* KJV

Faith is nothing
at all tangible.
It is simply
believing God.

Hannah Whitall Smith

It's All About Trust

People who promise things that they never give are like clouds and wind that bring no rain.

— *Proverbs 25:14 GNT*

Faithfulness in little things is a big thing.

Saint John Chrysostom

"But, Mom—you promised!" Nick complained.

"I know," Sherry answered. "But something came up."

Sherry looked down at the salad she was preparing as Nick stormed from the room. *It's not like I meant for this to happen*, she consoled herself. *I just forgot about it.*

But the next morning, Sherry thought about the Little League game she'd promised to attend—but hadn't. She remembered promising Nick that he could have his friends in for a sleepover—but she never planned it. Sherry had intended to carry through on lots of promises, but she hadn't.

A wave of guilt swept across Sherry's heart. She loved her son, but she knew she was failing him. *I'll make it up to him somehow*, she promised herself.

16

Sherry loved her child. But she was blind to the real cause of her dilemma until she faced the fact that her biggest problem wasn't a lack of time, energy, or money. It was a lack of credibility. She allowed distractions to keep her from following up on her word. Keeping your promises to your children is about more than just escaping guilt and feeling good. It's about building trust.

TRY THIS: *Save the word promise for sure things like "I promise I'll always love you." For the rest, make a plan rather than a promise. Sit down with your child and work out the particulars, making sure that he or she understands the difference. Then post your plans on the family calendar.*

IT IS A TRAP FOR A MAN TO DEDICATE SOMETHING RASHLY AND ONLY LATER TO CONSIDER HIS VOWS.

PROVERBS 20:25 NIV

HE WHOSE WALK IS BLAMELESS . . . KEEPS HIS OATH EVEN WHEN IT HURTS.

PSALM 15:2, 4 NIV

It is better to run the risk of being considered indecisive, better to be uncertain and not promise, than to promise and not fulfill.

OSWALD CHAMBERS

17

Time to Hear

The LORD has given us eyes to see with and ears to listen with.

— *Proverbs 20:12 GNT*

THE FIRST
DUTY OF LOVE
is to listen.
PAUL TILLICH

"Mom, I need to talk to you," twelve-year-old Mindy pleaded. "It's important."

Jan smiled. "Sure honey, just let me put these groceries away and start dinner." Two hours later, Jan was still racing from one chore to the next with no break in sight.

After dinner, Mindy tried again. This time Jan was on the phone lining up other mothers to teach Vacation Bible School. Mindy tugged on Jan's sleeve and mouthed the words, "Mom, please." But Jan, placing her hand over the mouthpiece said, "Sorry, honey. I'll be through here in just a minute."

When Jan's "minute" stretched into an hour, Mindy finally gave up and went to her room. Jan didn't notice. She was so busy being a great mom that she wasn't aware that she had neglected to be a good mom, a listening mom who takes time to find out what's up with her child.

🌿 Whether you work in the home or out of the home, keeping up with the everyday minutiae of raising a family can be challenging. That's why it's so important to keep things in perspective. Years from now, VBS and home-cooked meals may be forgotten, but the time you spent listening to your children could have lasting results. From your example, they will learn to listen to the important voices in their lives—yours, God's, and perhaps their children's.

🌿 TRY THIS: *Create listening time by asking your child to help with such tasks as making the salad, setting the table, helping fold clothes, or running errands with you. These settings are naturals for spontaneous conversations and can make it easier for your child to open up to you on tough topics.*

It is the province of knowledge to speak, and it is the privilege of wisdom to listen.
OLIVER WENDELL HOLMES

PERFECT KIDS

Arrogance will bring your downfall, but if you are humble, you will be respected.

— *Proverbs 29:23* GNT

Kathy and Devon were exceptional kids — no doubt about it. They were destined to be perfect kids if their mother, Judy, had anything to say about it. She kept the two elementary students dressed in the trendiest clothes, equipped with the newest toys and gadgets, and enrolled in the most prestigious private school.

But beneath the highly glossed veneer, problems loomed. Judy noticed that her children were becoming demanding, rude, and disrespectful. She was chagrined to see them treat their peers with disdain, and she was saddened when they shrugged off a gift from their uncle. They acted as if they resented her, despite all she was doing for them.

One Sunday, the pastor at her church spoke on the topic of pride, and Judy saw herself and her actions in their true light. Her quest for perfect kids was really a campaign to show others that she was the perfect mother.

Pride seldom uses its own name. If it did, you could easily spot it and put an end to its destructive ways. Instead, it's a chameleon, pretending at times to be love, courage, success, and other positive character traits. Pride whispers in your ear that your actions are selfless, your intentions pure, and your goal beneficent. Beat pride at its own game by embracing humility, its equal and opposite force.

Try this: *Make a conscious effort to notice how often you tell others about your own, or your children's, accomplishments — not because anyone has asked, rather because you're looking for their praise. Say good things about your children, of course, but whenever you find yourself bragging, change the direction of the conversation.*

When pride comes, then comes disgrace, but with humility comes wisdom.

PROVERBS 11:2 NIV

Before destruction one's heart is haughty, but humility goes before honor.

PROVERBS 18:12 NRSV

Just as darkness retreats before light, so all anger and bitterness disappear before the fragrance of humility.

JOHN CLIMACUS

21

Staying the Course

When the storm has swept by, the wicked are gone, but the righteous stand firm forever.

— *Proverbs 10:25 NIV*

"Football just isn't fun anymore," Trevor grumbled. It was late, and he had just come home after a rugged practice.

"I know it's taking up a lot more of your time than you'd planned," Trevor's mother, Karen, empathized. "We discussed this before you tried out for the team. But we have already paid all the fees, and you have made a commitment. You need to finish out the season."

As Trevor headed up the stairs, every footstep thudded in protest. Karen sighed. She could understand why football didn't seem like fun any more. But Karen also knew that it was important for Trevor to learn to keep working when things got tough. Quitting was rarely a solution.

"Lord," Karen prayed silently, "please show me how to encourage Trevor when his enthusiasm fades. I don't want to nag him. Show me how to persevere right along with him when he'd rather just give up. Help us hang in there together."

Endurance is simply pushing yourself a little farther than you think you can go and then doing it again. And again. And again. Life offers plenty of opportunities to surrender in the face of difficulty. The key to endurance is tackling it as a team sport. As a mom, relating to your child's struggle to do the right thing, as well as offering verbal, physical, and spiritual support, can mean the difference between giving up and going on.

TRY THIS: *When your child faces challenging circumstances and is tempted simply to give up, have an "endurance" celebration. Gather the family together and throw a party in the midst of discouragement. Write a congratulatory note. Hang an encouraging banner. Be creative in communicating your support. Let your child know that you notice his or her accomplishment.*

IF YOU ENDURE WHEN YOU DO RIGHT AND SUFFER FOR IT, YOU HAVE GOD'S APPROVAL.

1 PETER 2:20 NRSV

THE SAYING IS SURE: IF WE HAVE DIED WITH HIM, WE WILL ALSO LIVE WITH HIM; IF WE ENDURE, WE WILL ALSO REIGN WITH HIM.

2 TIMOTHY 2:11-12 NRSV

To endure is the first thing that a child ought to learn, and that which he will have the most need to know.

JEAN JACQUES ROUSSEAU

23

A Mother's Hope

H "Hope" is the thing with feathers

that perches in the soul

And sings the tunes without the words

And never stops at all.

Emily Dickinson

The hope of the righteous shall be gladness

— *Proverbs* 10:28 KJV

May the God of hope fill you with all joy and peace as you trust in him, so that you may overflow with hope by the power of the Holy Spirit.

— *Romans* 15:13 NIV

THE FUTURE IS AS BRIGHT AS THE PROMISES OF GOD.

ADONIRAM JUDSON

How Much Is Enough?

Obey the LORD, and you will live a long life, content and safe from harm.
— *Proverbs 19:23* GNT

Kara headed to the toy store before leaving the mall. She enjoyed this ritual. *I just love to see the kids' faces when I surprise them with a little something,* she thought. But then Kara's mind flashed to the reception she'd received from the kids last week.

"You didn't bring us anything? Anything at all!" Kevin and Jessica had whined. It was the day before payday, and the budget was still reeling from the car repairs the week before. Even a few dollars would have been a strain. But that hadn't mattered to the kids, and they had made their resentment obvious.

Kara realized that her gifts, intended to show love, had been sending her children the wrong message. *Today I'll give them a better gift—an opportunity to be content with what they have,* she thought. *I'll sit down and play with them—and help them enjoy something they already have—a mom who loves them.*

Living in a land of plenty, where wants often masquerade as needs, it can be puzzling to know how much is truly enough. It's perfectly all right to treat yourself or your kids to an occasional special indulgence, but those indulgences can be harmful if they leave your children discontented and demanding. Teach your children to live contented lives by helping them recognize the blessings God has already brought to their lives.

TRY THIS: *Each night, when you say prayers with your children, have them choose two things that they already have and thank God specifically for those two things in their prayers. Place no restrictions on their choices. The list might include things like: my mom, my bike, my best friend, the stars in the sky.*

SUCH IS THE END OF ALL WHO ARE GREEDY FOR GAIN; IT TAKES AWAY THE LIFE OF ITS POSSESSORS.

PROVERBS 1:19 NRSV

IF WE HAVE FOOD AND CLOTHES, THAT SHOULD BE ENOUGH FOR US.

1 TIMOTHY 6:8 GNT

It is so important not to waste what is precious by spending all one's time and emotion on fretting or complaining over what one does not have.

EDITH SCHAEFFER

I Was Wondering?

Listen to advice and accept instruction, that you may gain wisdom for the future.

~ *Proverbs 19:20* NRSV

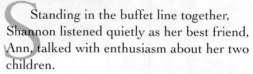

It can be no dishonor to learn from others when they speak good sense.

Sophocles

Standing in the buffet line together, Shannon listened quietly as her best friend, Ann, talked with enthusiasm about her two children.

"Connor and Lauren are such great kids. I couldn't be prouder," Ann said. "Every day I'm filled with wonder at the way they're growing and developing into such fine people."

Shannon headed for the desserts. *If only I felt that way about my kids,* Shannon thought. Her three children were young, and she often felt overwhelmed by motherhood and unsure of herself. *How can I ever feel the way Ann does?*

"How did you do it?" Shannon asked timidly as Ann joined her near the chocolate cake. "What did you do for your kids to help them turn out so well?"

Ann paused, with serving spoon in midair. "Some days were harder than others, but most of all I just hung in there, loved, and prayed," she said. "Maybe we could talk about it sometime over tea."

Motherhood isn't an exact science. There are no guarantees that what you do will produce the results you hope and pray for. Asking for advice along the way from other mothers who have walked more than a mile in your heels can give you needed strength and direction for the journey. Add in a few good parenting books, the wise advice found in the Bible, and plenty of prayer to be well equipped for the awesome task God has set before you.

TRY THIS: *Ask yourself if there is an older woman whom you respect as a mom. Then ask her out for lunch. Pick her brain over what she felt she did right, what she would change if she could, and how she made it through the hard times with her family and faith intact.*

WISE PEOPLE LISTEN TO ADVICE.

PROVERBS 12:15 GNT

WITHOUT COUNSEL, PLANS GO WRONG, BUT WITH MANY ADVISERS THEY SUCCEED.

PROVERBS 15:22 NRSV

Advice is like snow; the softer it falls, the longer it dwells upon, and the deeper it sinks into the mind.

SAMUEL TAYLOR COLERIDGE

I Mean It This Time!

Discipline your children, and they will give you rest; they will give delight to your heart.

~ *Proverbs* 29:17 NRSV

"Brandon, for the last time—pick up the junk you left in the basement!" Sue demanded. She had already told him three times.

"Sorry, Mom," Brandon said, heading toward the front door. "I promised the guys I'd meet them downtown. I'm already late."

Brandon was out the front door before Sue had time to protest. Sue clenched her jaws. She'd been fighting the same battle since Brandon had been a toddler. Then it was over putting away his toys; now it was over any chore Brandon thought interfered with his adolescent freedom.

Sue headed for the basement. Her friends would be there any minute. She didn't want them to see the disarray. As Sue carried the dishes and empty pizza boxes up the stairs, she paused at the kitchen. Then she continued up to Brandon's room and placed the whole mess on Brandon's bed. *Enough words,* Sue said to herself. *It's time for action.*

No matter how old your children are, while they are in your care you are responsible for helping to guide them to maturity. Discipline is an essential tool toward this goal and can't be neglected. Withholding discipline is detrimental and can delay a child's emotional growth. Resist the urge to rescue your children from the consequences of their own immature actions. Love your children and discipline them consistently and wisely.

TRY THIS: *Before enforcing any disciplinary action with your kids, put yourself in a momentary time-out. Check your motives. Are you acting out of anger or disciplining out of the desire to help your kids mature? Pray for wisdom in what action to take and what words to say. Then follow through with it, finishing up later with a hug.*

CORRECTION AND DISCIPLINE ARE GOOD FOR CHILDREN.

PROVERBS 29:15 GNT

NO DISCIPLINE SEEMS PLEASANT AT THE TIME, BUT PAINFUL. LATER ON, HOWEVER, IT PRODUCES A HARVEST OF RIGHTEOUSNESS AND PEACE FOR THOSE WHO HAVE BEEN TRAINED BY IT.

HEBREWS 12:11 NIV

I think of discipline as the continual everyday process of helping a child learn self-discipline.

FRED ROGERS

WHAT IF?

Worry can rob you of happiness, but kind words will cheer you up.

~ *Proverbs 12:25* GNT

For almost five years, Lesley and Dan prayed that they would be able to conceive a child. They could barely contain their excitement when they learned Lesley was pregnant. Nine months later, they were filled with joy as they held their beautiful daughter, Ashleigh. Unfortunately, in Lesley's mind also came the torturous thought, *What if?*

In the months ahead, worry kept Lesley awake at night. She panicked each time Ashleigh spit up or bumped her head or ran a slight fever. Each time the baby was out of her sight, the what-ifs overwhelmed her.

Finally, Dan suggested they pray together, and Lesley quickly agreed.

"Lord, thank you for Ashleigh," Dan prayed. "We entrust her to you and turn our backs on worry. Now help us as we make those words real in our everyday lives." It took awhile for Lesley to overcome her impulse to worry, but with God's help, she learned to trust.

32

Your instinct as a mother to protect and care for your child is God given. Without it, your helpless child might not survive. But that instinct becomes worry when it begins to turn inward and focus on you rather than on your children—what would you lose? how would you feel? Worry is born of an instinct to protect yourself rather than your children. Surrender those self-centered thoughts to God, and you will find yourself better able to enjoy your children.

Try this: *Combat worry and the what-ifs with this positive statement: "My children are not my own, they are God's. He is with them, even when I am not. He is protecting them, even when I cannot." Write out this statement and put it on your vanity mirror and on a card to place in your Bible.*

Whoever trusts in the Lord will be enriched.

Proverbs 28:25
NRSV

Don't worry about anything, but in all your prayers ask God for what you need, always asking him with a thankful heart.

Philippians 4:6 GNT

You can't change the past, but you can ruin the present by worrying about the future.

Author Unknown

A Mother's Love

Love feels no burden,

Thinks nothing of trouble,

Attempts what is above its strength,

Pleads no excuse of impossibility;

For it thinks all things lawful for itself,

And all things possible.

Thomas à Kempis

Love forgives all offenses.

— *Proverbs* 10:12 GNT

God is love, and those who live in love live in union with God and God lives in union with them.

— *1 John* 4:16 GNT

ACCUSTOM YOURSELF CONTINUALLY TO MAKE MANY ACTS OF LOVE, FOR THEY ENKINDLE AND MELT THE SOUL.

SAINT TERESA OF AVILA

What Really Matters

Those who trust in their riches will wither, but the righteous will flourish like green leaves.

— *Proverbs 11:28 NRSV*

"I don't have any money!" Joey moaned. "Everyone else is heading out to the climbing wall tonight. Couldn't you just lend me ten bucks until next week?"

On the surface it seemed like a reasonable request, and Carol knew how important it was for fifteen-year-olds to hang out with their friends on a Friday night. She also knew Joey would have had enough money if he hadn't spent his allowance the day after he had received it on fast food and video games.

"How about you help me clean out the garage for the next couple of hours?" Carol replied with a smile. "I could use the help and would pay you five bucks an hour."

Joey wasn't thrilled. But he sure hated the thought of his friends having an exciting Friday night without him.

"I guess," Joey said. "But why do I have to do so much work? Couldn't you just give it to me?"

Managing money can be daunting for people of all ages, and that's an excellent reason for teaching financial responsibility to your children early in their lives. Living within your means is a learned skill and, at the same time, a responsibility. It takes prayer, planning, and self-control to make money last from one period to the next. Teach your children while they are young to budget their allowance, spend wisely, give thoughtfully, and save for the future.

Try this: Help your children learn to handle money wisely by giving them hands-on training. When they're small, give them cash to buy a friend's birthday gift. Then help them stay within the budget. As they get older let them purchase the weekly groceries, their own school clothes, and even budget for the family vacation—all within the financial limits you set.

THE RICH AND THE POOR HAVE THIS IS COMMON: THE LORD IS THE MAKER OF THEM ALL.

PROVERBS 22:2 NRSV

WHY DO YOU SPEND YOUR MONEY FOR THAT WHICH IS NOT BREAD, AND YOUR LABOR FOR THAT WHICH DOES NOT SATISFY?

ISAIAH 55:2 NRSV

There is no wrong with people possessing riches. The wrong comes when riches possess people.

BILLY GRAHAM

Choosing Carefully

Godly people are careful about the friends they choose.

~ Proverbs 12:26 NIrV

Emily met Beth at choir practice for the community-wide Christmas pageant. At first it seemed they would be great friends. They were close to the same age, were married, and had three children in elementary school. Plus they both shared an interest in singing.

It wasn't long before Emily began to see things about Beth that concerned her. Beth indulged her children until they were whiny and demanding, and then she scolded and belittled them loudly. Beth also used sarcasm when talking about her husband and criticized him in front of their children.

Emily prayed about the situation and once tried to discuss the issues, but Beth didn't see things in the same way and just laughed them off.

Emily hoped that one day Beth would be able to overcome the character flaws that Emily felt plagued Beth's life. Until then, Emily decided she would have to look elsewhere for friendship.

Children are influenced by their friends, and they are influenced by your friends as well. Choosing godly friends who will set a good example for your children is a responsibility of great importance. And choosing friends who will encourage you to maintain a good attitude and proper respect for others is vital as well. Sometimes that means having the fortitude to walk away from certain relationships.

TRY THIS: *When you meet someone new, spend some time with her alone before you get together with your children. Share a long lunch at a restaurant or get involved in an activity that allows for conversation. Then listen. You will know pretty quickly if that person exhibits attitudes and behaviors that would be detrimental to you and your children.*

WE took sweet counsel together, and walked unto the House of God in Company.

PSALM 55:14 KJV

DON'T GO AROUND WITH A PERSON WHO GETS ANGRY EASILY. YOU MIGHT LEARN HIS HABITS. AND THEN YOU WILL BE TRAPPED BY THEM.

PROVERBS 22:24–25 NIrV

Let him have the key to thy heart who hath the lock to his own.
SIR THOMAS BROWNE

Safekeeping

The LORD provides help and protection for those who are righteous and honest. He protects those who treat others fairly, and guards those who are devoted to him.

~ Proverbs 2:7–8 GNT

GOD IS THE PROTECTOR OF THE BELIEVERS; HE BRINGS THEM FORTH FROM THE SHADOWS INTO THE LIGHT.

KATHE KOLLWITZ

"I'm sorry, David, but you're just going to have to live with my decision," Lisa said. "River rafting is out."

Lisa watched as anger and disappointment washed away David's cheerful smile. David grabbed his homework and headed for the den, his shoulders slumped. Lisa sighed. She knew her own fear of the water played a major part in her decision. The thought of David trapped beneath an overturned raft was more than Lisa could handle. *I have a responsibility to protect my son*, she told herself.

Lisa also knew what God would say— "David's life is ultimately in my hands, not yours."

"Lord," she prayed, "help me to overcome my fears and release my sweet son to your love and care. Help me to rid myself of irrational thoughts and replace them with calming thoughts."

"David," Lisa said, following her son into the den. "Let's sit down here and talk for a minute—tell me about this rafting trip."

40

Good moms protect their kids before they get in harm's way. They keep knives out of their reach, make sure their seat belts are buckled, and keep their vaccinations up to date. But there are limits to a mom's power. Being a good mom begins with recognizing this truth. Your children are only on loan to you. They belong to God. God can watch over them every moment wherever they go.

Try this: Picture your children as tiny, flightless birds, under your protection in the nest. Below the nest, picture God's tender, yet almighty, hands. Spend time in prayer over what this image brings to mind. Ask God to help your heart trust that if your children fall, he will be there to catch them.

WHOEVER LISTENS TO ME WILL LIVE IN SAFETY AND BE AT EASE, WITHOUT FEAR OF HARM.

PROVERBS 1:33 NIV

GOD WILL COVER YOU WITH HIS WINGS; YOU WILL BE SAFE IN HIS CARE; HIS FAITHFULNESS WILL PROTECT AND DEFEND YOU.

PSALM 91:4 GNT

The simple truth is that our children are safer in God's care than in our own.

ANDREA GARNEY

WHAT LIES IN THE HEART

All deeds are right in the sight of the doer, but the LORD weighs the heart.

~ *Proverbs 21:2 NRSV*

When Deirdre descended the stairs, Kelly could barely believe what she was seeing. Deirdre's combination of fuchsia shorts with bright flowers and lime tank top with a swirled and striped pattern grated against Kelly's sense of style like fingernails on a blackboard. "Wouldn't you rather wear your white T-shirt?" she asked.

"But, Mom," Deirdre protested, "I like this shirt. I look like a garden with flowers and leaves growing together. Isn't it pretty?"

Kelly took another look at her six-year-old's electric ensemble and smiled. Deirdre had definitely achieved a unique look. Kelly realized that even though she would be embarrassed to go out in such an outfit, Deirdre saw it differently. Kelly's uneasiness about the outfit was a product of concerned pride—what would the other mothers might think of her?—rather than of concern for her daughter.

"You know what, sweetheart," Kelly said, "you're absolutely right. What could be more lovely than a garden?"

"What's your motivation?" is a question that actors often ask themselves as they prepare to play a role. It's also a great question to ask yourself as you set limits for your kids. Along with your sincere love, wisdom, and concern, motivators such as fear, pride, shame, and selfishness also play a part in your decisions. Uncovering these hidden motives takes honest self-examination. Eliminating them requires God's guidance and a willingness to change.

Try this: *Write "What's my motivation?" on a 3" x 5" card. Tape it to your bathroom mirror or someplace else where you will see it often. Use this as a reminder to ask yourself that question as situations arise throughout your day. Note any insights you gain and ask God for guidance in contemplating any change.*

All one's ways may be pure in one's own eyes, but the Lord weighs the spirit.

Proverbs 16:2 NRSV

The Lord searches every mind and understands every plan and thought.

1 Chronicles 28:9 NRSV

I have four things to learn in life: to think clearly without hurry or confusion; to love everybody sincerely; to act in everything with the highest motives; to trust in God unhesitatingly.

Helen Keller

A Mother's Integrity

Thou must be true thyself
If thou the truth wouldst teach;
Thy soul must overflow if thou
Another's soul wouldst reach.

Speak truly, and each word of thine
Shall be a fruitful seed;
Live truly, and thy life shall be
A great and noble creed.

Horatius Bonar

The righteous walk in integrity—happy are the children who follow them!

— *Proverbs* 20:7 NRSV

The integrity of the upright shall guide them.

— *Proverbs* 11:3 KJV

THERE IS NO SUCH THING AS A MINOR LAPSE OF INTEGRITY.

TOM PETERS

THEIR EYES ARE ALWAYS WATCHING

Teach children how they should live, and they will remember it all their life.

— *Proverbs 22:6 GNT*

"You're eight miles over the speed limit, Mom," Jason noted. "Our driver ed instructor said, 'The speed limit is the speed limit, no matter how big a hurry you're in.' "

"I know," Sue sighed. "But if we don't make it to that checkup on time, they'll cancel our appointment."

Sue was about to explain to Jason how important it was to keep with the flow of traffic when she spotted a police car in her rearview mirror. Her foot immediately—and instinctively—tapped the brake. Her automatic reaction brought color to Sue's cheeks. How could she be a positive example of a responsible driver for her son when she was willing to bend the traffic laws to suit her situation?

"You know what Jason?" Sue asked her son. "You're absolutely right, and you're wise to pay attention to your instructor. The speed limit is the speed limit, no matter how big a hurry you're in."

When it comes to being a mom, actions really do speak louder than words. The fact that your children are likely to imitate your every move, the ones you're proud of as well as the ones you wish they hadn't seen, is a big responsibility. It is also a ready-made opportunity. Knowing you have an audience can open your eyes to habits that could use a little extra prayer and attention.

TRY THIS: *Make a list of character traits you'd like to see in your children as adults —such as honesty, compassion, discipline, or spiritual maturity. Ask yourself how well you measure up to the list you've made. Are there any areas you'd like to model more effectively? If so, ask for God's help in changing your habits and heart attitudes.*

EVEN CHILDREN SHOW WHAT THEY ARE BY WHAT THEY DO.

PROVERBS 20:11 GNT

IN ALL THINGS YOU YOURSELF MUST BE AN EXAMPLE OF GOOD BEHAVIOR.

TITUS 2:7 GNT

A good example is the tallest kind of preaching.

AFRICAN CHIEF

The Simple Truth

A lie has a short life, but truth lives on forever.

~ *Proverbs 12:19* GNT

"I can't play because I have to clean my room," Kaye heard her son, Bradley, say to someone at the front door. Kaye walked to the entry hall in time to see a sad-faced young boy shuffle away. As Bradley closed the door, he was surprised to find his mother standing behind him.

"You have to clean your room, huh?" Kaye asked. She knew he had already made his bed and put away all his books and toys.

"Mom, Ben isn't fun at all," Bradley said. "He always gets mad at me when we play together. I don't want to play with him."

"Not wanting to play with him is one thing," Kaye said. "Lying about it is another. Why don't we ask God to give you the right words to say to Ben? Maybe he needs someone to ask him why he gets mad all of the time. If you like, we could ask him together."

🌿 The words that come out of people's mouths are like plants in a garden. Their speech can be filled with flowers or overgrown with weeds. Habits such as exaggeration, false flattery, or stretching the truth to save face are signals that the heart needs a little yard work. Asking God to help you pull up lies by their dishonest roots is not only good for your own heart, but it also gives your kids a positive example to emulate.

🌿 TRY THIS: *Memorize Proverbs 30:8, "Keep falsehood and lies far from me." Use this verse as a short prayer to God each day for the next month. Ask God to reveal any untruthful habits that may have taken root in your own life. Then ask for his help in replacing these weeds with verbal flowers of truth.*

DO NOT LET KINDNESS AND TRUTH LEAVE YOU.

PROVERBS 3:3 NASB

BUY THE TRUTH AND DO NOT SELL IT; GET WISDOM, DISCIPLINE AND UNDERSTANDING.

PROVERBS 23:23 NIV

Honesty has a beautiful and refreshing simplicity about it. No ulterior motives. No hidden meanings. An absence of hypocrisy, duplicity, political games, and verbal superficiality.

CHARLES R. SWINDOLL

ALL IS NOT LOST

Sometimes it takes a painful experience to make us change our ways.

~ *Proverbs 20:30 GNT*

Connie shook her head. Both Tyler and Hannah were in their rooms with instructions to think about their answer to her question. *All I want to know is what happened to the twenty dollar bill in my wallet. I know it didn't just disappear on its own.* Yet both denied having any knowledge about the twenty.

Having two kids in junior high was straining the budget, and Connie knew both kids had been pushing for a raise in their allowance. *They've always been such honest kids,* Connie thought. *I can't imagine either of them doing anything like this.*

Just then Connie's husband walked in from work. "Hey, Hon, sorry I'm late," he said, kissing her on the cheek. "Oh yeah . . . I borrowed twenty dollars from your wallet for lunch this morning. Hope it wasn't a problem."

Connie's heart sank. *I blew it big time,* she reprimanded herself. *I'd better head upstairs and set things right.*

50

Mistakes are the construction zones of life that make you slam on the brakes and ask yourself, "What's going on here?" They are reminders that everyone, no matter how young or old, is a work in progress. For God to complete his work in your heart, you have to be willing to risk making mistakes and to learn from them, no matter where you are on life's journey.

Try this: *When you need to apologize to your kids, take a moment to explain what you've learned from your mistake. In turn, when your kids blow it, ask them what God has taught them through their blunders. Finish by taking a moment together to thank God that he is perfect, even when his children are not.*

If you listen to advice and are willing to learn, one day you will be wise.

Proverbs 19:20 GNT

Learn prudence; acquire intelligence, you who lack it.

Proverbs 8:5 NRSV

Learn from the mistakes of others—you can't live long enough to make them all yourself.

Martin Vanbee

51

Inside My Head

The LORD detests the thoughts of the wicked, but those of the pure are pleasing to him.

— *Proverbs* 15:26 NIV

OUR LIFE IS
WHAT OUR
THOUGHTS
MAKE IT.
SAINT CATHERINE
OF SIENA

The kids are in bed, Ron's working late, and here I am with a movie, a bowl of popcorn, and some time just for me, Sarah thought contentedly. *Who could ask for more?*

But within a few minutes, Sarah found herself asking for more. Although the movie had gotten good reviews and her friends had recommended it, Sarah wasn't happy with it. She wanted more humor and fewer sick jokes, more love and less sex, more hope and less cynicism. She wanted more meaning, a story God would write—and this certainly was not.

With one click of the remote the TV faded to black. The stillness that followed was welcome and unexpectedly comforting. Sarah smiled, closed her eyes, and prayed, *Lord, thank you for the longing you've put in my heart to fill my mind with what's pleasing to you. Guide me in what's right and pure, and make me more like you.*

It's easy for a train of thought to jump the tracks and careen downhill. It's important to guard what goes into your mind and what you spend time meditating on. Even if your actions are well intentioned, if your thoughts are contrary to God's design, you'll miss out on the peace, joy, and contentment he's planned for you. Nothing is as exciting as living out the unique adventure God has in store for you alone.

TRY THIS: *When you sit down to watch a movie or TV show, with or without your kids, picture God sitting right next to you. Would he enjoy what you're watching? If having God see what you're putting into your mind makes you uncomfortable, turn off the TV or leave the theater. Don't give your mind the opportunity to jump the track.*

FILL YOUR MINDS WITH THOSE THINGS THAT ARE GOOD AND THAT DESERVE PRAISE.

PHILIPPIANS 4:8 GNT

A TRANQUIL MIND GIVES LIFE TO THE FLESH.

PROVERBS 14:30 NRSV

Change your thoughts and you change your world.
NORMAN VINCENT PEALE

A Mother's Peace

There is a life deep hid in God
Where all is calm and still,
Where, listening to His holy Word,
One learns to trust, until
All anxious care is put away
And there is peace, profound, always.
Grant us Thy peace, O God!

Henry W. Frost

*Those who counsel peace
have joy.*

— *Proverbs* 12:20 NRSV

*Those of steadfast mind
you keep in peace — in
peace because they trust
in you.*

— *Isaiah* 26:3 NRSV

IF THE BASIS OF
PEACE IS GOD, THE
SECRET OF PEACE
IS TRUST.

J. N. FIGGIS

Letting It Go

When someone wrongs you, it is a great virtue to ignore it.
~ *Proverbs* 19:11 GNT

Lula was in the kitchen when she heard the sound of breaking glass coming from the living room. Rushing toward the sound, she spotted her four-year-old twins, their eyes staring unbelievingly at the pieces that littered the floor. The ball in the entryway told the story. Chad and Chris had broken Lula's grandmother's favorite plate playing catch in the house, again.

"To your rooms," Lula said with quiet intensity. "Now."

As the boys left the room, Chad hesitated, and then turned to face his mother. With tears in his eyes he said, "You forgive me?"

Hanging behind him, Chris said, "Me too?"

Lula looked at them both, brushing away tears of her own. She knew it had been an accident, albeit one that wouldn't have happened had her sons obeyed her. "Yes, Chad, Chris," Lula said. "I forgive you. So does God. Why don't you talk to him about it while you're up in your room?"

Motherhood will offer you countless opportunities to give your children a priceless gift—your forgiveness. But this gift doesn't come without a price. To extend it freely, you'll have to sacrifice something. It could be your pride, your resentment, your anger, or your pain. By putting this unattractive sacrifice into God's hands, he enables you to forgive those who've hurt you. God has done the same for you—and has asked you to follow in his footsteps.

Try this: Take fifteen minutes to sit quietly with God and ponder his forgiveness. Think back on your life. What are some of the things God has forgiven you? Is there anyone you need to extend forgiveness to? Consider the depth of God's grace and the sacrifice it took for him to share that grace with you and your family. Offer him your heartfelt gratitude.

Jesus said, "Forgive us the wrongs we have done, as we forgive the wrongs that others have done to us."

Matthew 6:12 GNT

Be kind to one another, tenderhearted, forgiving one another, as God in Christ has forgiven you.

Ephesians 4:32 NRSV

It is by forgiving that one is forgiven.

Mother Teresa

Not a Chance!

Those who guard their way preserve their lives.

~ *Proverbs 16:17 NRSV*

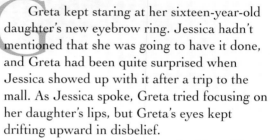

Greta kept staring at her sixteen-year-old daughter's new eyebrow ring. Jessica hadn't mentioned that she was going to have it done, and Greta had been quite surprised when Jessica showed up with it after a trip to the mall. As Jessica spoke, Greta tried focusing on her daughter's lips, but Greta's eyes kept drifting upward in disbelief.

Now, what do I say? Greta asked herself. Then her mind flashed back to her own sixteenth year—bell bottoms, go-go boots, love beads, fishnet stockings—and the cheap perm she'd gotten behind her mother's back. Her best friend's hair had come out looking like spirals of silk. But Greta's dark brown, cropped locks had resembled some type of lightning-struck rodent. So much for feeling like one of the beautiful people.

"Let's talk about why this is so important to you," Greta said to Jessica in deliberately calm tones. "Then let's talk about how very important you are to God—and to me."

The purpose of camouflage is to blend in with your surroundings. Succumbing to peer pressure is one way of doing just that. This kind of camouflage isn't always beneficial, for either kids or adults. Acting like those around you eventually will no longer be an act. It will become a habit. The more you and your children emulate God's character, the more you'll be able to stand out in a crowd and be secure in the person God has created you to be.

TRY THIS: When your kids go out with friends, take just a moment to pray for the influence each of these friends will have on the lives of your children. Ask God to protect your children from any negative influences, as well as to help your children be a positive, godly influence in the lives of those around them.

SENSIBLE PEOPLE ALWAYS THINK BEFORE THEY ACT.

PROVERBS 13:16 GNT

PAY ATTENTION TO WHAT YOU ARE TAUGHT AND YOU WILL BE SUCCESSFUL.

PROVERBS 16:20 GNT

Yes and no are the two most important words that you will ever say.

AUTHOR UNKNOWN

Safely Abiding

You will walk on your way securely and your foot will not stumble. If you sit down, you will not be afraid.

— *Proverbs* 3:23–24 NRSV

In all of her daydreams about motherhood, Bonnie had pictured herself as the happy, confident mother. But she was numb with anxiety as she sat by her baby's tiny hospital bassinette. The only emotion that seemed to penetrate the nightmare was fear—the fear of losing the little boy she'd waited nine months to meet.

Fear wasn't something Bonnie usually had to battle. Typically, living life on the edge energized her. But right now, all Bonnie wanted was the assurance that everything would be all right.

Fear not . . . the words an angel spoke to frightened shepherds on the night of another birth two thousand years ago kept echoing through her mind.

God, I know you love Gavon even more than I do, Bonnie prayed through her tears. *But I'm afraid I'm going to have to say good-bye before I hardly have a chance to say hello. How do I "fear not" at a time like this?*

🌿 Life is filled with circumstances that can incite fear in the most courageous of hearts. Learning to "fear not" is more than a matter of keeping a stiff upper lip or living in denial. It's a matter of trusting that the God who loves you will never leave your side. His plans and answers to prayer may not be what you have in mind, but embrace the knowledge that he is in control and promises to bring good out of every circumstance.

🌿 TRY THIS: *Create your own artwork for the refrigerator. Draw a picture of God's arms, open wide, reaching out in love for you and for each one of your children. Write everyone's name on the drawing, and use this drawing as a reminder that God's plans are bigger than your own.*

THOSE WHO WALK IN WISDOM COME THROUGH SAFELY.

PROVERBS 28:26
NRSV

BE STRONG AND DON'T BE AFRAID! GOD IS COMING TO YOUR RESCUE.

ISAIAH 35:4 GNT

The chains of love are stronger than the chains of fear.

WILLIAM GURNALL

SETTING THE TONE

A cheerful look brings joy to the heart.

~ *Proverbs 15:30 GNT*

A CHEERFUL
LOOK MAKES A
DISH A FEAST.
GEORGE HERBERT

The doorbell chime set off momentary chaos. Ginger the dachshund scurried toward the front door through the kitchen at the same time Bridget was heading to the table with the gelatin salad. She stepped on Ginger's paw, Ginger let out a yelp, and the salad landed flat on the floor.

So much for the perfect lunch, Bridget thought to herself, as the lemon gelatin swayed and wobbled on the freshly scrubbed linoleum. The ladies in her Bible group would see this when she opened the door. Bridget wanted to cry. She'd planned this luncheon for a week.

"Funny, Mommy! Funny!" Shannon giggled with two-year-old glee.

Something in Bridget's heart softened. *Shannon is right. It is funny.* Bridget realized she had a choice— hang on to her irritation, which would put a damper on lunch with her friends, or let go and laugh at herself. *There's really only one choice to make*, Bridget thought, hurrying to the door with a welcome grin.

A cheerful home is a place of welcome for both family and friends. Even when circumstances are less than perfect, there is great joy in knowing that God can bring something good out of every situation, big or small. That's the true foundation of a positive attitude. So if you want a cheerful home filled with cheerful hearts, the first attitude check you need to make is on your own. Your attitude is contagious, and your children will pick up on it.

Try this: To raise the cheerful quotient in your home, make laughter a regular part of your family's healthy habits. Be prepared to share one new joke every evening around the dinner table. Encourage your children to do the same. When chaos and tension threaten the peace, you may want to double the daily dosage.

A CHEERFUL HEART IS GOOD MEDICINE.

PROVERBS 17:22 NIV

BEING CHEERFUL KEEPS YOU HEALTHY. IT IS SLOW DEATH TO BE GLOOMY ALL THE TIME.

PROVERBS 17:22 GNT

Wondrous is the strength of cheerfulness, and its power of endurance.

THOMAS CARLYLE

A Mother's Strength

Father in Heaven, my strength is so small

Sometimes, it feels like I have none at all.

I struggle and groan as I make my way

To shoulder my burden for one more day.

Then I remember that your arms are strong

And you're always willing to help me along.

So, Father, I give my great burden to You

And thank You for doing

what I could not do.

ANDREA GARNEY

The way of the LORD is strength to the upright.

— *Proverbs* 10:29 KJV

God gives strength to the weary and increases the power of the weak.

— *Isaiah* 40:29 NIV

WHEN GOD IS
OUR STRENGTH, IT
IS STRENGTH
INDEED; WHEN
OUR STRENGTH IS
OUR OWN, IT IS
ONLY WEAKNESS.

SAINT AUGUSTINE
OF HIPPO

Doing My Best

The desires of the diligent are fully satisfied.

~ *Proverbs 13:4* NIV

Few things are impossible to diligence and skill.

Samuel Johnson

The sound of Colin's colicky cry woke Paige from a deep sleep. She glanced at the clock—2:38 A.M.—and struggled to put on her robe. Paige had already repeated this ritual four times since crawling into bed at 11:15 P.M. She was exhausted, and the night wasn't even half over.

Paige gathered her five-week-old son into her arms, whispering, "It's okay, sweetheart, it's okay." She wasn't sure whether she meant for her words to reassure Colin or to encourage her own heart. But they seemed to do both.

Taking care of her crying newborn as well as her two older children left Paige feeling as though there was not enough of her to go around. Tonight, though, Paige's heart was overcome with praise. She'd never felt more thankful that God was with her, moment by moment, giving her the strength she needed to keep going. *Lord, thanks for reminding me just how much I need you,* she whispered.

66

A mom's diligence is determined by her many jobs accomplished with excellence. It is measured by how much of her heart she gives to the task at hand. Choosing to give yourself physically, emotionally, and mentally to any job, particularly one as intense as motherhood, takes focus and dependence on the One who enables you to accomplish with excellence whatever task he sets before you.

TRY THIS: *When you spend time with your kids, whether it's nursing your baby, enjoying a family vacation, or reading a bedtime story, make a conscious effort to be involved mentally, physically, and emotionally. Begin by putting any unfinished tasks or personal concerns into God's hands. He'll hold them until you have time to give them your full attention.*

THE PLANS OF PEOPLE WHO WORK HARD SUCCEED.

PROVERBS 21:5 NIRV

THE HAND OF THE DILIGENT MAKES RICH.

PROVERBS 10:4 NRSV

For the diligent the week has seven todays; for the slothful seven tomorrows.

AUTHOR UNKNOWN

Walking in God's Ways

Even children make themselves known by their acts, by whether what they do is pure and right.

— *Proverbs* 20:11 NRSV

Whereas obedience is righteousness in relation to God, love is righteousness in relation to others.

A. Plummer

"It's only one day off from school, and we're not doing much right now," Jenna pleaded. "Lindsey's mom lets her take a mental health day every couple of months. I just need some time to veg out."

"I understand you're tired," Beth said, looking Jenna in the eye. "But I can't tell the school you're sick. You're not. If you want to take the day off as an unexcused absence, that's one thing, but I won't lie for you."

"An unexcused absence would stay on my record, Mom," Jenna said. "I don't want to do that."

"Then, I guess you'll have to go," Beth said. "Honey," she added, "there are plenty of times I'd rather stay home in my pajamas and read a good book, but that wouldn't be the right thing to do. Choosing to do the right thing isn't always easy, but it's God's choice, and that makes it mine, too. I know that'll be your choice as well."

Not all rules are easy, or pleasant, to follow. They may even feel constraining, unfair, or downright unnecessary at times. When it comes to knowing right and wrong, your children need to be taught the purpose of rules and laws and how they contribute to a civilized, God-fearing society. Whether the rules are traffic laws, family curfews, or the Ten Commandments, their aim is the same—to protect.

TRY THIS: Play "What Would God Do?" with your kids. Brainstorm different life scenarios where the right answer isn't easily apparent. For instance, ask "If God saw someone he loved cheating on a test, what would he do?" or "If God received a CD as a gift and he didn't like some of the lyrics on it, what would he do?"

THE LORD BLESSES THE ABODE OF THE RIGHTEOUS.

PROVERBS 3:33 NRSV

IN THE WAY OF RIGHTEOUSNESS IS LIFE; AND IN THE PATHWAY THEREOF THERE IS NO DEATH.

PROVERBS 12:28 KJV

Clothe yourself with the silk of piety, with the satin of sanctity, with the purple of modesty, so shall God Himself be your suitor.

QUINTAS TERTULLIAN

GOD WILL REPAY

Don't take it on yourself to repay a wrong. Trust the LORD and he will make it right.

~ *Proverbs 20:22* GNT

Ginnie jumped out of her car, feeling like a mother grizzly bear bounding off to care for her defenseless cub. Ginnie wasn't sure what to do first—console her sobbing seven-year-old daughter or catch the bully who had grabbed her backpack and then thrown it to the ground.

Before Ginnie could make it across the playground, she saw the culprit escape onto a school bus. Ginnie's mind and emotions were racing as she watched the bus pull away from the curb. Hurrying toward Emma, Ginnie prayed, *Lord, how do Emma and I love someone like that little bully Morris? Help me to have a loving attitude.*

After all, it wasn't the first time Morris had picked on Emma or her friends. Morris's nickname Morris the Terrorosaurus had been well-earned on the elementary school playground. As Ginnie and her daughter walked to the car, Ginnie asked God to soften the heart of an angry little Terrorosaurus.

When people in your children's lives are less than kind, the world will tell you it's payback time. God offers a radically different approach. The Bible says to pray for your enemies, and it goes even farther—it says to love them. That's because true love replaces revenge with forgiveness. Forgiveness is a gift that benefits the giver even more than the one on the receiving end.

Try this: The way to love and forgive someone who's hurt you begins with prayer. Think of someone who has treated you badly. Commit to pray for that person every morning for two weeks. Pray for insight into what loving this person should look like, and then ask for the perseverance to follow through on what you've learned.

If your enemies are hungry, feed them; if they are thirsty, give them a drink.

PROVERBS 25:21 GNT

Don't be glad when your enemies meet disaster, and don't rejoice when they stumble.

PROVERBS 24:17 GNT

If we could read the secret history of our enemies, we should find in each life sorrow and suffering enough to disarm all hostilities.

HENRY WADSWORTH LONGFELLOW

It Doesn't Feel Right

Keep your faith and a clear conscience.

~ *1 Timothy 1:19* GNT

"Don't take it the wrong way or anything," Samantha said. "I'd just feel more comfortable staying home. Have fun and take care, Shannon. Bye." Samantha hung up the phone and turned to find her mom standing behind her.

"I didn't mean to overhear," Cherie commented, "but did you say you weren't going to Shannon's tonight? That doesn't sound like you. May I ask why you don't want to? You two always get together on Friday nights."

Samantha hesitated. Then she said, "Shannon's folks are out of town, and she's invited lots of kids from school over to her house, guys and girls. Some of them I don't even know. It just didn't feel right to me."

At that moment, Cherie thought how much more grown-up her daughter seemed than sixteen. "You know something?" Cherie asked Samantha. "It takes a mature woman to listen to her conscience even when her friends may not understand. I'm really proud of you."

What some people call "women's intuition" is often your God-driven conscience. It's a personal guidance system that helps you stay away from situations that may not be in your best interest. As your heart becomes more like God's, you want to turn away from anything that has the potential to dishonor him. Talk to your children about the importance of listening to God's still, small voice before they make decisions.

Try this: *If your smoke detector goes off, you immediately check it out. You ask yourself, "Is there really a fire?" or "Does it just need new batteries?" When the alarm of your conscience goes off, do the same thing—check it out. Ask yourself, "What does God think of this situation?" "What would he want me to do?"*

Who can say, "I have kept my heart pure; I am clean and without sin"?

PROVERBS 20:9 NIV

The LORD gave us mind and conscience; we cannot hide from ourselves.

PROVERBS 20:27 GNT

Conscience tells us in our innermost being of the presence of God and of the moral difference between good and evil.

BILLY GRAHAM

A Mother's Benevolence

It is not the weight of jewel or plate,

Or the fondle of silk or fur;

'Tis the spirit in which the gift is rich,

As the gifts of the Wise Ones were,

And we are not told whose gift was gold,

Or whose was the gift of myrrh.

Edmund Vance Cooke

*A generous person
will be enriched, and one
who gives water
will get water.*

— *Proverbs* 11:25 NRSV

*If you are eager to give,
God will accept your gift on
the basis of what you have
to give, not on what you
don't have.*

— *2 Corinthians* 8:12 GNT

A CHEERFUL GIVER
DOES NOT COUNT
THE COST OF WHAT
SHE GIVES. HER
HEART IS SET ON
PLEASING AND
CHEERING THE ONE
TO WHOM THE
GIFT IS GIVEN.

JULIAN OF NORWICH

Thy Will Be Done

When good people pray, the LORD listens.

— Proverbs 15:29 GNT

The sound of the mail truck pulling away from her house always made Gillian smile. Gillian looked forward to the surprise of magazines, catalogs, and, best of all, an occasional letter from a friend. Today Justin's report card drew Gillian's eye.

School had always been a struggle for Justin. Last semester's report card had certainly shown evidence of that. This semester they'd decided to try something different. In addition to Justin's usual tutoring, Gillian and her son had set aside time each morning before school and each afternoon before homework to petition God for his help. Justin had been hesitant at first. He questioned whether God even wanted to bother with something that was so small to God. But after a few weeks, Justin looked forward to the time as much as Gillian did.

As Gillian unfolded the report card, another smile crossed her lips. Today she and Justin would take time for both petition and praise.

Prayer is a cry of the heart. Some cries may be painful, yet others are joyous, loving, and full of praise. Regardless of the emotion behind the cry, God is always there, listening to hear what his beloved child has to say. Just as earthly friendships deepen through honest conversation, so also does your relationship and communication with God draw you closer to him.

Try this: *Make prayer for your children a regular part of your life. Once a week, sit down with your children individually and ask what struggles and concerns you can pray about for them for the coming week. Use that time also to ask what God did in response to things you prayed for during the previous week.*

DEVOTE YOURSELVES TO PRAYER, BEING WATCHFUL AND THANKFUL.

COLOSSIANS 4:2 NIV

THE PRAYER OF THE UPRIGHT IS HIS [GOD'S] DELIGHT.

PROVERBS 15:8 NRSV

The purpose of all prayer is to find God's will and to make that will our prayer.

CATHERINE MARSHALL

Guess What I Heard

No one who gossips can be trusted with a secret, but you can put confidence in someone who is trustworthy.

— *Proverbs* 11:13 GNT

The girls chatted away in the back of the van. Ellen tried not to listen in, but it was impossible to block out their conversation. Once her daughter and her friends started talking, they seemed to forget that she could hear and drive at the same time.

"Gordon passed me a note in English," one friend bragged to her junior-high peers. "He said Andrea cheated on the test. He saw her looking at someone else's paper. Can you believe it?"

The back of the van erupted with preteen gasps: "Andrea?!" "No way!" "Are you sure?" "I thought so." "Did I tell you what her best friend told me?" "No wonder she gets such good grades."

Ellen's shoulders grew tense. As she pulled into the school's parking lot to drop the girls off for soccer practice, she turned and waved the girls to stay put. "Before you go dashing out of here," she began, "let's talk about what I just heard."

78

Keeping communication positive means that you are able to discern the difference between solving a problem and spreading gossip. That discernment begins by asking God for wisdom. It continues by sharing your concerns only with those who are part of the problem or part of the solution—and making absolutely certain you have your facts straight. Then you're free to share words of hope and healing, instead of rumor and hearsay.

TRY THIS: *Pray about sharing a personal story with another and examine your motives before doing it. Even sharing something personal and then asking others to pray about it can be a way of spreading gossip. Ask God to prick your conscience when you are tempted to say something you shouldn't.*

A WHISPERER SEPARATES CLOSE FRIENDS.

PROVERBS 16:28
NRSV

A GOSSIP CAN NEVER KEEP A SECRET. STAY AWAY FROM PEOPLE WHO TALK TOO MUCH.

PROVERBS 20:19
GNT

Do not listen gleefully to gossip at your neighbor's expense or chatter to a person who likes to find fault.

MAXIMUS THE CONFESSOR

This Will Be Fun!

Let the wise listen and add to their learning.

— *Proverbs 1:5 NIV*

"There were dinosaurs and rocks and stuffed cheetahs and even a place where you got to walk inside a human body!" Douglas excitedly recounted some of the adventures he'd experienced at the Museum of Natural History.

"Wow! You'd think you'd taken your kids to an amusement park," Julia commented to Douglas's mom, Carla. "It sure sounds like they had a great time!"

Carla nodded. "They did, and I did too. It was fabulous." Carla told Julia all the things kids could do at the museum and everything that she'd learned that morning—right down to the function of a gall bladder. "You sound almost as excited as Douglas!" Julia laughed.

"You know, I probably am!" she responded. "My mom took me to a lot of museums as a kid. She always said, 'Learning something new about life is learning something new about God!' What could be better than that? We're going to be going back. That's for sure!"

80

Children spend much of their young lives asking why, and inquisitive and growing moms keep right on doing that very same thing. They stimulate their children's curiosity about the world and God's hand in it. That's how a love of learning is passed from one generation to the next. Nurturing your own curiosity can help you keep a sense of wonder while increasing your children's interest in school and whetting their appetites for a deeper understanding of God.

INTELLIGENT PEOPLE WANT TO LEARN.

PROVERBS 15:14 GNT

TRY THIS: *Ask each person in your family to talk about one skill he or she would like to try. This could be something as simple as making an origami crane or as difficult as learning to speak a bit of Chinese. Schedule a family day for each learning adventure. Then encourage everyone to participate.*

APPLY YOUR HEART TO INSTRUCTION AND YOUR EARS TO WORDS OF KNOWLEDGE.

PROVERBS 23:12 NIV

Learning is not attained by chance. It must be sought for with ardor and attended to with diligence.

ABIGAIL ADAMS

Hopping from Friend to Friend

Friends always show their love.

— *Proverbs* 17:17 GNT

"Bye, Mom," Emily yelled down the hallway. "I'll be at Brittney's for a couple of hours or so."

Teresa came out of the kitchen, a dishcloth still in her hand. "I thought you were going to see Madison tonight," Teresa remarked. "This afternoon you said you were going to her volleyball game to cheer her on."

Sixteen-year-old Emily played absentmindedly with her car keys. "Yeah, well, that's before I knew Brittney was having a party," Emily said, a little sheepishly. "I didn't even know about it until the last minute. Mom, I'm sure Madison would do the same thing if she had a chance to go."

Teresa put her arm on Emily's shoulder. "I'm not sure she would, but that's not really the point, is it? The point is, Madison would probably be disappointed to look into the bleachers and not find you there."

Constancy is one vital characteristic that makes God's love trustworthy. God's love for you doesn't change according to whim or circumstance. His promises and compassion remain steadfast today, tomorrow, and until the end of time. In human relationships, a reflection of that kind of faithful love is found in the virtue of loyalty. Being loyal to your spouse, your friends, and your children lets them know they can trust you and your word. That kind of trust grows one honorable decision at a time.

TRY THIS: *Make a list of the top five relationships in your life, including the one with God. Then take out your calendar for the coming week. In light of your schedule, ask God to show you any commitments you need to add, juggle, or drop so that you can spend some time with the people who mean so much to you.*

THOSE WHO PLAN GOOD FIND LOYALTY AND FAITHFULNESS.

PROVERBS 14:22
NRSV

HE THAT IS FAITHFUL IN THAT WHICH IS LEAST IS FAITHFUL ALSO IN MUCH.

LUKE 16:10 KJV

Love and loyalty are a mother's unconditional gifts to her children.

SUSAN HAFER

A Mother's Goodness

If you do good,

People may accuse you of selfish motives.

Do good anyway.

The good you do today

May be forgotten tomorrow.

Do good anyway.

Author Unknown

The good leave an inheritance to their children's children.

~ *Proverbs* 13:22 NRSV

Live as children of light—for the fruit of the light is found in all that is good and right and true.

~ *Ephesians* 5:8-9 NRSV

AN ACT OF GOODNESS, THE LEAST ACT OF TRUE GOODNESS, IS INDEED THE BEST PROOF OF THE EXISTENCE OF GOD.

JACQUES MARITAIN

I Need a Hug

Let love and faithfulness never leave you; bind them around your neck.

~ *Proverbs 3:3 NIV*

Two-year-old Garrett toddled in from the backyard, an air of urgency in his awkward steps, to the kitchen where Donna was sitting with her friend. Through sobs, tears, and gasps, Garrett finally managed to point a pudgy finger toward the two children left playing on the slide.

While what had happened outside was uncertain, one message was undeniably clear. Garrett stood before his mother on tiptoe, his arms stretched high above his head. This was Garrett's silent plea that Donna had come to understand long before Garrett could even talk. Donna wrapped her son in her arms, held him close to her heart, and whispered, "Mommy's here." She kissed him and brushed away his tears.

As Donna rocked Garrett gently in her arms, she was struck by the thought, *How straightforward Garrett is. He knows what he needs and he asks for it. How comfortable do I feel asking for a hug when I need one?*

❧ Love is an action verb that is expressed whenever you meet the needs of another person. One of those needs is physical touch. Cherishing or comforting another physically is one way of putting flesh on the arms of an invisible God. God has given you the privilege of holding your children close, hugging and embracing them for him until he can do the same for them in heaven.

❧ TRY THIS: *Make a habit of surprising your kids with a hug for no special reason, other than that you love them. If you establish this practice at an early age, it's easier to continue this type of affection throughout the teenage years, when your kids are less likely to ask for a hug when they need it.*

LOVE ONE ANOTHER WARMLY AS CHRISTIANS, AND BE EAGER TO SHOW RESPECT FOR ONE ANOTHER.

ROMANS 12:10 GNT

HE TENDS HIS FLOCK LIKE A SHEPHERD: HE GATHERS THE LAMBS IN HIS ARMS AND CARRIES THEM CLOSE TO HIS HEART; HE GENTLY LEADS THOSE THAT HAVE YOUNG.

ISAIAH 40:11 NIV

Affection is responsible for nine-tenths of whatever solid and durable happiness there is in our lives.

C. S. LEWIS

Meeting Their Needs

Do what is right and fair; that pleases the LORD more than bringing him sacrifices.

~ Proverbs 21:3 GNT

HOLD YOURSELF
RESPONSIBLE FOR
A HIGHER
STANDARD THAN
ANYBODY ELSE
EXPECTS OF YOU.
HENRY WARD
BEECHER

Jenna lifted Amy's curls to fasten the golden locket around her neck. As she did, Jenna thought back to her own thirteenth birthday, when her mother had fastened the necklace around Jenna's neck. How thrilled she had been to be one in a line of Miller women who had the privilege of wearing this necklace.

"This was originally your great-grandmother Colette's," Jenna said. "It's over a hundred years old, and now it's yours. If you have a daughter, when she turns thirteen you can pass it on to her. See? Inside the heart is a tiny engraved cross. It's a reminder of how much you're loved by Jesus and by me."

"I'll take care of it, Mom," Amy said. "I'll keep it safe. I promise."

"With privilege comes responsibility." Jenna's mother's often-repeated words echoed through her mind. *Lord,* Jenna prayed, *I know the privilege of being Amy's mom. Help me live up to the responsibility.*

Parenting is one of the greatest privileges life affords. As your children grow and you experience all the responsibility that this entails, you will find yourself trusting God more and more for his help. Praying for God's wisdom, and relying on his promise to be a guide and protector for your children, is a source of courage that will never fail.

Try this: *Instead of assigning your children chores, make it clear you are entrusting them with responsibilities. When they receive greater family responsibilities, grant them greater privileges. Do this on a regularly scheduled basis—quarterly, for instance. Top it off with a family celebration where new responsibilities and privileges are presented in a positive way.*

GUARD WHAT HAS BEEN ENTRUSTED TO YOU.

I TIMOTHY 6:20
NRSV

DO YOUR BEST TO PRESENT YOURSELF TO GOD AS ONE APPROVED BY HIM, A WORKER WHO HAS NO NEED TO BE ASHAMED.

2 TIMOTHY 2:15
NRSV

The most important thought I ever had was that of my individual responsibility to God.

DANIEL WEBSTER

THE B-I-B-L-E

Those who respect the commandment will be rewarded.

~ *Proverbs 13:13* NRSV

"Jonah ran away?" Drew asked through tears.

"He knew what God wanted him to do," Darla explained, "but he was afraid to do the right thing—just like you." Darla ran her fingers tenderly through Drew's hair as she continued. "I know you're afraid to tell Sean you liked his new car so much that you put it in your pocket when he wasn't looking."

"Can I just give it back?" Drew sobbed. "Can I just put it on his front porch and not tell him who did it?"

Darla understood what Drew was going through. She also knew how easy it would be to set things right on the outside without dealing with the inside. "The Bible says that Jonah finally stopped running away. He told God he was sorry. I think you can be as brave as Jonah. I think you can knock on Sean's door and apologize. Why don't we ask God to help you?"

Motherhood is filled with teaching moments—and the Bible is an excellent textbook. The Bible is a love letter to you and your children from God and is filled with advice on how to live and with encouragement on how much you are loved. The better you know God and his Word, the more you will find yourself using the Bible as a resource and comfort as you meet the challenges of raising your children.

TRY THIS: *Watch the movie The Ten Commandments as a family. Spend time afterward talking about the life of Moses. Discuss why he had the faith to do what he did. Then ask your children how they might have acted in his place. Would they have had the courage to stand up to Pharaoh? Lead the people out of bondage?*

EVERY WORD OF GOD IS FLAWLESS.

PROVERBS 30:5 NIV

THE WORD OF GOD IS QUICK, AND POWERFUL, AND SHARPER THAN ANY TWO-EDGED SWORD.

HEBREWS 4:12 KJV

If our children have the background of a godly, happy home and this unshakeable faith that the Bible is indeed the Word of God, they will have a foundation that the forces of hell cannot shake.

RUTH GRAHAM

Light My Path

The human mind plans the way, but the LORD directs the steps.

— *Proverbs 16:9* NRSV

DEEP IN YOUR
HEART IT IS NOT
GUIDANCE THAT
YOU WANT AS
MUCH AS A
GUIDE.

JOHN WHITE

"Two acceptance letters!" Karen beamed as her eyes skimmed the university stationery. "I'm so proud of you."

"But, Mom!" Trina cried, "What should I do? I really like Virginia Tech, and it has the work-study program I need. But the University of Virginia is offering me a partial scholarship and is closer to home. On the other hand, Virginia Tech is smaller." Trina dropped to the couch, overwhelmed by the weight of the decision before her. "I wish only one college had accepted me," Trina said. "It would have been so much simpler. How do I know which is the right school for me?"

"We can ask God for guidance. Why don't we do that right now," Karen said, taking her daughter's hands. "Lord, Trina's future is in your hands, and she needs your guidance. Direct her steps, Lord. Lead her in the direction you want her to go. Show me what I can do to help. Amen."

When God created you and your children, he gave each of you free will. That means your lives are filled with choices. Some of them are almost inconsequential—paper or plastic?—while others are life-altering—who will you marry? What career path will you follow? If a decision is big enough to weigh on your mind and heart, it's big enough to bring to God. He promises to give wisdom freely to anyone who asks.

TRY THIS: *When you need to make a decision big enough to pray about in your life, involve your kids. You don't need to share every detail, just that you need God's help in knowing which way to go. Ask them to pray for you, and with you. Then ask if you could pray for any areas in which they need guidance.*

REMEMBER THE LORD IN EVERYTHING YOU DO, AND HE WILL SHOW YOU THE RIGHT WAY.

PROVERBS 3:6 GNT

I GUIDE YOU IN THE WAY OF WISDOM AND LEAD YOU ALONG STRAIGHT PATHS.

PROVERBS 4:11 NIV

It is morally impossible to exercise trust in God while there is failure to wait upon Him for guidance and direction.

D. E. HOSTE

A Mother's Kindness

Spread love everywhere you go:

First of all in your own house.

Let no one ever come to you without

Leaving better and happier.

Be the living expression of God's kindness;

Kindness in your face, kindness in your eyes,

Kindness in your smile,

Kindness in your warm greeting.

Mother Teresa

Kind words are like honey—sweet to the taste and good for your health.

— *Proverbs* 16:24 GNT

As God's chosen ones, holy and beloved, clothe yourselves with compassion, kindness, humility, meekness, and patience.

— *Colossians* 3:12 NRSV

A KIND HEART IS A FOUNTAIN OF GLADNESS, MAKING EVERYTHING IN ITS VICINITY FRESHEN INTO SMILES.

WASHINGTON IRVING

Think Before You Act

Folly is a joy to one who has no sense, but a person of understanding walks straight ahead.

— *Proverbs* 15:21 NRSV

The backpack had everything a middle school boy could want—including a pocket for Jarrod's CD player and a special strap for his skateboard. The brand name and the Skateboard Association's official logo on the flap was probably why the backpack cost sixty dollars—thirty dollars over what Jarrod and his mom had agreed to spend.

"I'm sorry, Jarrod," Cindy told her son. "All you really need is something to get your books to and from school. Thirty bucks. That's it. That's the budget we agreed on before we left home."

Jarrod started to protest. "But, Mom . . ." His heart had been set on the spiffier backpack since he'd spotted it in the store's special display. In contrast, the thirty-dollar backpack was serviceable but plain. Then it occurred to him: he would be paying twice as much simply to have the strap and the logo, worth maybe three dollars extra at the most. He grinned. *No way, man!*

Common sense is frequently learned through trial and error. The book of Proverbs is filled with common sense that otherwise would have to be learned through life's hard knocks. The advice in Proverbs is simple and direct, and its advice is forever enduring. The more familiar you become with it, the more you will be able to pass its pragmatic wisdom on to your children.

Try this: Share a proverb at the dinner table at least once a week. Select a contemporary Bible version that is especially suitable for children, such as the New International Reader's Version or the Good News Translation. Talk about what the proverb means and why the advice it gives is good. As a family, come up with a practical situation where you could apply the "common sense" shared in the proverb.

SENSIBLE PEOPLE ACCEPT GOOD ADVICE.

PROVERBS 10:8 GNT

SENSIBLE PEOPLE WILL SEE TROUBLE COMING AND AVOID IT.

PROVERBS 22:3 GNT

Faith is believing in things when common sense tells you not to.

GEORGE SEATON

WATCH WHAT YOU SAY

If you want to stay out of trouble, be careful what you say.

~ *Proverbs 21:23* GNT

HANDLE THEM
CAREFULLY, FOR
WORDS HAVE
MORE POWER
THAN ATOM
BOMBS.

PEARL STRACHAN

"How do you think your words made Kevin feel?" Ann bent down to look her five-year-old daughter in the eye. Cassie shrugged her shoulders and stared at her shoes. "Would you think it was all right if Mommy said something like that to you? How would it make you feel?"

Cassie looked up, her eyes growing wider and filling with tears. "You'd never call me that, would you?" Cassie said. "You love me."

"That's right," Ann continued. "And I know you love Kevin. Being the big sister isn't always easy, but Kevin looks up to you—and listens to you. I know that you love him, and I think he needs to hear just how much you care."

Cassie needed no further prompting. Whispering a soft "Sorry, Mommy," Cassie went off to find her brother. Ann smiled. *Lord,* she prayed, *help me be just as careful with my words as I'd like my children to be.*

Once something is spoken it can never be revised or erased. That's why it is important to take the time to think before you speak. At times, choosing the right words may actually mean choosing to say nothing at all. This can be difficult when you are engaged in a heated exchange fueled by anger, gossip, or frustration. Ask God to help you make each word a gift to the person who hears it.

TRY THIS: *Give your children at least one special gift of words a day. These should be above and beyond the usual parental compliments. Say what your children may not hear anywhere else. Share deep truths, such as what you love about them, how creatively God designed them, or why the world is a better place because they are in it.*

A GOOD PERSON'S WORDS WILL BENEFIT MANY PEOPLE.

PROVERBS 10:21 GNT

AVOID PROFANE CHATTER, FOR IT WILL LEAD PEOPLE INTO MORE AND MORE IMPIETY.

2 TIMOTHY 2:16 NRSV

Words which do not give the light of Christ increase the darkness.

MOTHER TERESA

GOD IS OUR HELPER

The LORD is like a strong tower, where the righteous can go and be safe.

~ *Proverbs 18:10* GNT

As the moving van pulled away, Julie's emphatic waving changed to uncontrollable sobbing. Dorothy scooped her young daughter into her arms, hugged her tightly, sat down with Julie on her lap, and rocked her gently.

"It's hard to say good-bye to a best friend," Dorothy said quietly, "especially when you're lucky enough to have one who lived next door. You can always be friends, honey. You can send letters and tell each other what you're doing."

"But, Mommy," Julie said shakily, "Dawn's moving so far away."

"Do you know what?" Dorothy said. "God will be right there with Dawn in Arizona, just like he's right here with us this very minute. He loves both of you even more than you love each other. That's why he wants to help. Let's ask God to help you and Dawn stay friends, even though you're far apart. And let's ask him to dry your tears from the inside out."

In the Psalms, God says he holds every one of your tears in a bottle. That means your heart cannot break without it affecting God. He cares about your pain, both physical and emotional, and offers his comfort any time of day or night. While the solace you offer your children is invaluable, teaching your kids how to reach out to God the Father will provide them with a source of comfort that can heal wounds far beyond your reach.

TRY THIS: *Give each of your children a capped bottle or jar half full of water to set on a shelf in their room. Explain to your children that when they are sad, God sees every one of their tears and wants to help take the pain away. Their bottles can serve as a reminder to tell God where it hurts.*

You, O LORD, have helped me and comforted me.

PSALM 86:17 NIV

PRAISE BE TO THE GOD AND FATHER OF OUR LORD JESUS CHRIST, THE FATHER OF COMPASSION AND THE GOD OF ALL COMFORT, WHO COMFORTS US IN ALL OUR TROUBLES.

2 CORINTHIANS 1:3–4 NIV

To need consolation and to console are human, just as human as Christ was.

DOROTHY SOELLE

101

It Hurts!

A glad heart makes a cheerful countenance, but by sorrow of heart the spirit is broken.

~ *Proverbs 15:13* NRSV

WE ARE HEALED OF GRIEF ONLY WHEN WE EXPRESS IT TO THE FULL.

CHARLES SWINDOLL

"Do turtles go to heaven?" Clayton asked his mom. He stared forlornly at the small burial site in the backyard.

"I don't really know what happens to turtles when they die," Candice replied. "I do know that God created so many different animals that he must really care about them. He is in God's hands now. I know how much you cared about Pokey. I'm sorry he died."

Clayton started crying all over again. "It hurts, Momma, it hurts!" Candice felt her own heart breaking along with Clayton's. "Why did he die, Momma?"

Candice knew words couldn't heal Clayton's heart. She put her arm around his shaking shoulders and called on the only one who had conquered death—and offered the hope of something beyond it. "Lord," Candice began, "you care for the sparrows, so I know that even a turtle matters to you, just as it does to Clayton. Heal Clayton's heart as only you can."

God created men and women to live eternally with him. Death interrupted this perfect design when people chose to rebel against the very one who would give anything, even his only Son, to show how much he loved them. When grief touches your family, God is the only one who offers true comfort. He is the Word when there are no words, the Healer when it appears all hope is gone.

TRY THIS: *Ask your children what they think heaven will be like—many rooms and a throne, for instance. Then look together at what the Bible has to say. A few passages of scripture to consider are John 14:2–3, 2 Corinthians 5:1, Philippians 3:20–21, Isaiah 65:17, and Revelation 4, 7:15–17, 21:1–7.*

MY FLESH AND MY HEART MAY FAIL, BUT GOD IS THE STRENGTH OF MY HEART AND MY PORTION FOREVER.

PSALM 73:26 NIV

JESUS SAID, "BLESSED ARE THEY THAT MOURN: FOR THEY SHALL BE COMFORTED."

MATTHEW 5:4 KJV

Grief can be your servant, helping you to feel more compassion for others who hurt.

ROBERT SCHULLER

A Mother's Patience

A mother waits with patience
As her child begins to walk,
Then coaxes very gently
As her child learns how to talk.
A mother waits with patience
As her child goes off to school;
She watches and she wonders,
Waiting calmly is the rule.
A mother waits with patience
For that's what mothers do;
Each step from childhood onward,
She sees her children through.

Victoria Parsons

*Patient persuasion
can break down the
strongest resistance.*

~ *Proverbs* 25:15 GNT

*If we hope for what we
do not yet have, we wait
for it patiently.*

~ *Romans* 8:25 NIV

HAPPY HOMES ARE
BUILT WITH
BLOCKS OF
PATIENCE.

AUTHOR UNKNOWN

Hopes and Dreams

et reverence for the LORD be the concern of your life. If it is, you have a bright future.

— Proverbs 23:17–18 GNT

PURPOSE IS WHAT GIVES LIFE MEANING. A DRIFTING BOAT ALWAYS DRIFTS DOWNSTREAM.

CHARLES PARKHURST

"But they all have long legs, Mom," Gretchen said forlornly. "I'm the shortest girl in ballet. Ballerinas are tall and pretty and graceful. And I'm just me." Gretchen sat down on her bed and cupped her chin with both hands.

"That's what I love most about you," Sharon replied. "You're just you, exactly the way God intended. I know your legs are like mine, not very long, but those legs will get you where God wants you to go. My legs got me where I needed to go. And don't forget—God is the one who gave you a heart that loves to dance."

"Does that mean I'll get to be a ballerina when I grow up?" Gretchen asked hopefully.

Sharon smiled. "I'm not sure what God has planned for you, honey," Sharon said, "but I know that whatever it is, he's going to be proud of you. Me too."

106

God knits every individual together in the womb with specific physical characteristics, strengths, weaknesses, talents, and tendencies. Then he gives each person one more thing—purpose. The desire to find your place in the world is a God-given drive that helps you to make the most of your own unique role in life. Though some roles receive more public accolades than others, all of God's children have starring roles.

Try this: In three to five sentences, write a mission statement for your life. Make sure your statement is specific and something you believe you can achieve with God's help. One of the sentences should reflect your relationship with God, one should reflect your relationship with your family, and one should reflect your personal desires.

A LONGING FULFILLED IS A TREE OF LIFE.

PROVERBS 13:12 NIV

THE APOSTLE PAUL SAID, "I PRESS ON TOWARD THE GOAL FOR THE PRIZE OF THE HEAVENLY CALL OF GOD IN CHRIST JESUS."

PHILIPPIANS 3:14 NRSV

God sees every one of us; He creates every soul . . . for a purpose.

JOHN HENRY NEWMAN

Full to Overflowing

Blessings crown the head of the righteous.

~ *Proverbs 10:6 NIV*

Jolene watched little Tyler's rhythmic breathing move his tiny chest up and down. Watching her baby sleep filled Jolene's heart with praise, which overflowed into a quiet chorus. "Praise God from whom all blessings flow . . ."

Jolene knew that she had clothes waiting to be laundered, bills waiting to be paid, and supper ready to be started. But right now she couldn't think of anything more important than thanking God for the not-so-little things—a long-awaited child, her family's health, a pantry filled with food, even the sunlight streaming through the half-open window. After kissing Tyler softly on the forehead, Jolene sat down, her back bathed in warmth of the afternoon sun, and closed her eyes.

"Father," Jolene prayed, "you're so good to me. Slow me down more often. Keep my eyes open wide enough to see your hand working in every corner of my life. As your blessings overflow, let my thanks do the same."

Blessings are marks of God's favor. And when a loving God pours his fullness into your life, you overflow with blessings. Whether in times of joy or sorrow, prosperity or need, God's blessings are evident. All you need is the ability to see them clearly. A thankful heart serves as the perfect pair of glasses to help you do just that. The more you give thanks, the more you notice how much you have to be thankful for.

Try this: *Make prayer before the evening meal more meaningful for your family by going around the table and having each person share one blessing God has brought his or her way during the course of the day. Then when you pray, thank God for all of these blessings, as well as for the food.*

The faithful will abound with blessings.

Proverbs 28:20
NRSV

How wonderful are the good things you keep for those who honor you! Everyone knows how good you are, how securely you protect those who trust you.

Psalm 31:19 GNT

The best things are nearest: breath in your nostrils, light in your eyes, flowers at your feet, duties at your hand, the path of God just before you.

Robert Louis Stevenson

Knowing God

Trust in the LORD with all your heart and lean not on your own understanding; in all your ways acknowledge him, and he will make your paths straight.

— Proverbs 3:5–6 NIV

Chad had a question for every page of his Bible storybook. "Mommy, why didn't that bush Moses saw burn up?" "How did Samson's hair make him stronger than anyone else?" "How did that little stone knock Goliath down?" "How could Jesus walk on water?"

"Because God can do anything," Jessica found herself saying over and over again. *With God nothing is impossible.* The verse came to Jessica's mind unbidden, but the question that followed it disturbed her. *Do I really believe that?*

Jessica tucked Chad into bed and made her way to the study, her mind filled with questions. Jessica had known God since she was Chad's age, but sometimes she felt her son's love for God was deeper than her own. *God, why do I believe what I believe?* Jessica pondered, then prayed. *I want to know you, and love you, more deeply. Please, show me how.*

One way to draw closer to your children is by reading the Bible together. It brings you face-to-face with God's character, and it draws a picture of the depth of his love and boundless limits of his power. Talking to God about what you read will draw you even closer, helping you trust him with all your questions—even those that may remain unanswered until you meet face to face.

TRY THIS: *As you read through the Bible, personalize it. Whenever God gives a promise, such as "I will never leave you nor forsake you," substitute your name for the word you. Put yourself in the shoes of those you read about and imagine that God is speaking those words directly to you.*

WHOEVER PURSUES RIGHTEOUSNESS AND KINDNESS WILL FIND LIFE AND HONOR.

PROVERBS 21:21
NRSV

DRAW NEAR TO GOD, AND HE WILL DRAW NEAR TO YOU. CLEANSE YOUR HANDS, YOU SINNERS, AND PURIFY YOUR HEARTS, YOU DOUBLE-MINDED.

JAMES 4:8 NRSV

There is a God-shaped vacuum in the heart of every man which cannot be filled by any created thing, but only by God, the Creator, made known through Jesus.

BLAISE PASCAL

Remember Who You Are

If you have to choose between a good reputation and great wealth, choose a good reputation.

— *Proverbs* 22:1 GNT

"It's just a shirt, Mom," Chandra said. "I think it's funny!"

Deb read her daughter's new T-shirt to herself one more time, DON'T PICK ME UP—YOU DON'T KNOW WHERE I'VE BEEN. Deb shook her head and sighed. "Chandra, I know you don't really mean anything by it, but that shirt conveys a message that I don't think you intend. It hints that you may have been places a Christian girl wouldn't go or done things a Christian girl wouldn't do," Deb said.

Chandra began to fidget uneasily as her mother's words sank in. "I'm so glad God chose you to be my daughter," Deb said. "But you're not only my child, you're God's. Everything about you, the way you dress, the way you talk, the way you act toward others—it's all a reflection of who you are. Be who you are, honey, that's all I ask. Don't suggest to others that you're something or someone you're not."

Consider the constant public scrutiny of Britain's royal family. People are always watching what they say, what they do, even what they wear. You and your children are also royalty. You are the sons and daughters of an almighty King. And people will be watching you as well. They will judge your reputation by what they see and hear. They may even judge the reputation of the King you serve based on what they see in you.

Try this: *As you wait in the line at the grocery store, use the tabloids as a prompt for prayer. Whenever you see a headline that talks about Britain's royal family, spend a moment thanking God for the royal heritage he's given you. Then ask him to point out any area in your life where your reputation could use a little help.*

The memory of the righteous will be a blessing.

Proverbs 10:7 NIV

A good name is better than fine perfume.

Ecclesiastes 7:1 NIV

Glass, china, and reputation are easily crack'd and never well mended.

Benjamin Franklin

A Mother's Encouragement

The soul of a child is the loveliest flower

That grows in the Garden of God;

Its climb is from weakness to

knowledge and power,

To the sky from the clay and the clod.

Be tender, O gardener, and give it its share

Of moisture, of warmth, and of light,

And let it not lack for thy painstaking care

To protect it from frost and from blight.

Author Unknown

A person's words can be a source of wisdom, deep as the ocean, fresh as a flowing stream.

— *Proverbs* 18:4 GNT

Encourage the timid, help the weak, be patient with everyone.

— *I Thessalonians* 5:14 NIV

CORRECTION DOES MUCH, BUT ENCOURAGEMENT DOES MORE. ENCOURAGEMENT AFTER CENSURE IS AS THE SUN AFTER A SHOWER.

JOHANN WOLFGANG VON GOETHE

FOR MY BODY'S SAKE

Fear the LORD, and turn away from evil. It will be a healing for your flesh and a refreshment for your body.

— *Proverbs 3:7–8 NRSV*

Barbara opened the freezer and surveyed the contents—a few TV dinners, chicken parts, ground beef, bags of mixed fruit, and packages of vegetables. It was the carton in the back of the freezer, however, that Barbara decided to call dinner.

"Mocha double fudge," Barbara said to herself with a smile. "The perfect meal—especially with Gary treating the kids to dinner at the game. H'm. Maybe some chocolate sauce, too."

Before the ice cream had made it the counter, however, Barbara was having second thoughts. *I'm always telling the kids how important it is to take care of the body God gave them. Do I really believe what I'm saying? Well, then, shouldn't I act on what I believe?*

Barbara opened the refrigerator, found the leftover pasta and salad, and returned the ice cream to the freezer. For now . . . she reassured herself. I'll see if I'm still hungry after I've eaten some real food.

116

Your body is a one-time gift from a loving God. However, it's a gift that requires constant maintenance. Making wise choices about the fuel you put into it, the rest and exercise you give it, and the regular check-ups you schedule for it are ways of saying thank you to God. As a mother, the way you take care of your own health speaks loudly to your children. Make sure you give them the message that you want them to hear.

Try this: *How long has it been since you've had a mammogram (if you're over forty), a pap smear, and a gynecological exam? If it has been more than two years, get on the phone and schedule an appointment. How long since you've evaluated the healthfulness of the foods you eat? Your diligence is a gift to God, your kids, and yourself.*

[GOD'S WORDS] ARE LIFE TO THOSE WHO FIND THEM. THEY ARE HEALTH TO YOUR WHOLE BODY.

PROVERBS 4:22 NIRV

I PRAY THAT EVERYTHING MAY GO WELL WITH YOU AND THAT YOU MAY BE IN GOOD HEALTH.

3 JOHN 2 GNT

Take care of your health, that it may serve you to serve God.

SAINT FRANCIS DE SALES

I Can Do This

Anyone who shows respect for the LORD has a strong tower.

~ Proverbs 14:26 NIrV

"I can't do it!" Jeremy declared adamantly.

"That's not what I think," Joan said. She stooped down to look her six-year-old son in the eye. "I think when you asked to jump off the diving board that it looked like a lot of fun. And do you know what? It is! What's more, I think you can do it. It takes courage to step off the edge. If you'd like, we can do it together, all three of us—you, me, and Jesus."

Jeremy's unfolded his arms and opened his eyes wide in surprise. "Really? Jesus would jump in the pool with me?" he asked his mom.

"You bet," Joan affirmed. "He'll never leave your side. He knows what a good swimmer you are, and he is ready to help you jump—even if it looks a little scary." Joan took Jeremy's hand, and he stepped forward. His smile had a new hint of confidence.

꧁ Knowing that God is with you and your children can give you the courage to step out and be who you were created to be. It can give you the courage to fail, then get up and try again. When fear tries to talk you out of doing something, don't listen. Instead, remind yourself of what God has to say about you—you are more than a conqueror through God who loves you (Romans 8:37).

꧁ TRY THIS: *Think of two things you would like to do but have not had the courage. This could be any number of things—introducing yourself to someone new, signing up for a class, learning to use your computer. Then strike out to do it, keeping in mind that God has given you the desire and he is with you each step of the way.*

THE LORD WILL BE YOUR CONFIDENCE.

PROVERBS 3:26 NIV

IN QUIETNESS AND CONFIDENCE SHALL BE YOUR STRENGTH.

ISAIAH 30:15 KJV

The greater and more persistent your faith in God, the more abundantly you will receive all that you ask.

ALBERT THE GREAT

OVER THE TOP!

Better a little with the fear of the LORD than great wealth with turmoil.
— *Proverbs 15:16 NIV*

THE PROCESS OF
LIVING IS THE
PROCESS OF
REACTING
TO STRESS.

STANLEY J. SARNOFF

It was still dark when Timmy started crying. Apparently Kristi's stomach flu had been contagious after all. Carmen got Timmy cleaned up and back in bed, threw a load of laundry in the wash, then went to wake up Taylor. That's when the grating sounds alerted her to the malfunctioning washer. Water was overflowing onto the floor she had just scrubbed yesterday. In her haste to clean the laundry room, she didn't get Taylor ready in time to catch the school bus.

By noon, Carmen already felt as though she'd put in a full day's work. She finally sat down with a cup of tea, and a smile crossed her lips. She'd made it. Carmen knew God understood what lay behind her smile. They'd had a running conversation through it all.

Time for a moment of thanks and rest, Carmen thought. *Then, I'll be ready for whatever this afternoon may hold.*

Like an eye in the midst of the storm, God's presence provides a peaceful oasis in the midst of chaos. The key is to take your eyes off the storm and to put them directly on him. When tension is running high, make it a point to pray and to recite Scripture. Picture God by your side helping and guiding you. God has the power to calm the storms that surround you as well as the ones brewing within you.

Try this: *When you feel stress starting to build, take a break. Find a quiet spot where you won't be disturbed and take a moment to sit quietly with God, asking for his peace and perspective. Take several deep breaths, praising God for his power in your life, each time you exhale. Repeat as needed.*

IN MY DISTRESS, I CALLED TO THE LORD, AND HE ANSWERED ME.

JONAH 2:2 NIV

O LORD, BE GRACIOUS TO US; WE LONG FOR YOU. BE OUR STRENGTH EVERY MORNING, OUR SALVATION IN TIME OF DISTRESS.

ISAIAH 33:2 NIV

Anxiety comes from strain and strain is caused by too complete a dependence of ourselves, on our own devices, our own plans, our own idea of what we are able to do.

THOMAS MERTON

A Reason to Rest

When you lie down, you will sleep soundly.

~ *Proverbs 3:24 NIrV*

As Peg crawled into bed, she could hear her husband's quiet breathing. He must have fallen asleep some time ago. She had been up for hours trying to lull Dennis, their three-year-old, back to sleep after he'd had a bad dream.

"But, Mommy, the story won't go away!" Dennis had told Peg. Peg knew exactly what he meant. At times her mind would keep reliving the details of a full day or rehearsing worries about what was awaiting her tomorrow. When those things crept vividly into her thoughts, getting the "story" to turn off wasn't something she was able to do on her own.

"Let Jesus tell you another story," Peg had assured her son. "Let him hold you close and sing you a lullaby about how much he loves you."

Now, as she snuggled next to her husband, it was Peg's turn to pull the comforter up around her ears and take her own advice.

Sleep is a gift, given by the very one who created your need for it. Motherhood can make your appreciation of that gift grow. Whether it's rocking a newborn, nursing a sick child, or waiting up for a teen to return from a late evening out, there are times your body will long for rest. When your energy wanes, or when you find yourself tossing and turning, turn to the God who never sleeps.

Try This: *When you have trouble sleeping, don't count sheep. Go straight to the shepherd himself. Picture yourself in his loving arms, handing over every care that's weighing heavy on your mind. As you let go of each one of your concerns, thank God that his hands are big enough to carry them all.*

THE SLEEP OF A LABORER IS SWEET.

ECCLESIASTES 5:12
NIV

IN VAIN YOU RISE EARLY AND STAY UP LATE, TOILING FOR FOOD TO EAT—FOR HE GRANTS SLEEP TO THOSE HE LOVES.

PSALM 127:2 NIV

We sleep in peace in the arms of God, when we yield ourselves up to his Providence.

FRANÇOIS FENELON

A Mother's Wisdom

Keep sound wisdom and prudence,

and they will be life for your soul

and adornment for your neck.

Then you will walk on your way securely

and your foot will not stumble.

If you sit down, you will not be afraid;

when you lie down, your sleep will be sweet.

PROVERBS 3:21–24 NRSV

Wisdom is a fountain of life to one who has it.

— *Proverbs 16:22* NRSV

It is better—much better—to have wisdom and knowledge than gold and silver.

— *Proverbs 16:16* GNT

KNOWLEDGE IS
THE POWER OF THE
MIND, WISDOM IS
THE POWER
OF THE SOUL.

JULIE SHANNAHAN

At Inspirio we love to hear from you—your
stories, your feedback,
and your product ideas.
Please send your comments to us
by way of e-mail at
icares@zondervan.com
or to the address below:

inspirio

Attn: Inspirio Cares
5300 Patterson Avenue SE
Grand Rapids, MI 49530

If you would like further information
about Inspirio and the products we
create please visit us at:
www.inspiriogifts.com

Thank you and God Bless!